T0146392

Corazón:

FROM THE HEART OF LATIN AMERICA

Corazón:

FROM THE HEART OF LATIN AMERICA

A *Documentary Journey* through
Mexico, Central America, and the Andes

W. R. Stanton

iUniverse®

CORAZÓN: FROM THE HEART OF LATIN AMERICA
A DOCUMENTARY JOURNEY THROUGH MEXICO, CENTRAL AMERICA, AND THE ANDES

iUniverse books may be ordered through booksellers or by contacting:

iUniverse
1663 Liberty Drive
Bloomington, IN 47403
www.iuniverse.com
1-800-Authors (1-800-288-4677)

ISBN: 978-1-5320-4082-5 (sc)
ISBN: 978-1-5320-4081-8 (e)

Library of Congress Control Number: 2018900801

Print information available on the last page.

iUniverse rev. date: 02/27/2018

CONTENTS

INTRODUCTION IX

THE ANDES I

GUAYAQUÍL 29

MEXICO CITY 37

OUTSIDE THE CAPITOL 47

THE YUCATAN 63

BELIZE 7I

EPILOGUE 77

Dedicated to

Lauren Llavín Kopel-Stanton

INTRODUCTION

"For me the camera is a sketchbook; an instrument of intuition and spontaneity; the master of the instant."

Henri Cartier Bresson

Will & Nancy Stanton: Chetumál, Quintana Roo 1989

My love affair with Latin America began with a bad map. I first traveled to Mexico in the late 60s, but only to the borderlands of Chihuahua and Sonora. My initial portal into that world was Sásabe, Arizona. Sásabe at that time was a tiny cowboy outpost with only a bare bones border crossing to El Sásabel, Sonora. It was way before the drug wars, the militarized border and nativist vigilantes on the American side, so the guy in the US customs shack just waved us through. On the Mexican side there was only a tiny wooden building with nobody in it. What the border people knew and we didn't was that there was nothing beyond El Sásabel but cow paths and dirt jeep tracks that went out into the desert. They all thought that we'd hang around El Sásabel for a while and come back. But we didn't.

We chose Sásabe to cross into Mexico because our Rand-McNally map book showed a paved road from the border to the town of Altár, about 100 km south. From Altár we figured we could drive west to Mexicali on Sonoran Route 2 and enter back into the US at Calexico, in the Imperial Valley of California. It was a good plan, except that there was no paved road from El Sásabel to Altár.

El Sásabel at that time consisted of dirt streets, two bars and a couple dozen adobe houses. We drove through slowly, expecting the pavement to begin at any moment. But all we saw at the end of town was Saguaro cactus marching out into the desert and a two-track jeep road heading south. We were driving a Volkswagen bus with good traction, had plenty of gas and water and figured the map might have been wrong about the road surface but not about the general direction. So we positioned the afternoon sun on the passenger side of the bus and drove south into the desert. What I remember about that stretch of landscape, other than the frequent washouts and the Saguaro, was that midway between the border and Altár there was a village. There was a communal well in the center of it, some goats wandering around and otherwise just silence. It was siesta time, so no humans were in sight: just the goats, the heat and us. More than forty years later I still think of that place often. I remember the starkness, the simplicity… and the stillness.

Later that afternoon we reached Altár, then drove west across the Sonoran desert. At dusk we reached Mexicali and talked our way back into the States. I remember the colors of the desert as we drove into the setting sun that day: the golds in the sky, the blacks of the formations in lee of the sun, the muted tans of the surrounding landscape. But there is no visual record of any of it, or of the trip from Sásabe to Altár. In fact, I didn't pick up a camera seriously until ten years later.

In the early 70s, I spent a year traveling with my first wife through Mexico, all of Central America and down through the Andes to Bolivia. During that year I became immersed in the richness of daily life, the tumultuous history and the cultural variety of life south of the U.S. border. When I returned to the states I got a job as an outreach worker with Latino farm workers in Massachusetts. By then I had been speaking Spanish every day for over two years. As my street Spanish improved I discovered that the physical act of speaking Spanish was different than when speaking English. My voice came from deeper in my chest and resonated more fully. My English was more cerebral and nuanced; my Spanish more visceral and animated. As my familiarity with the culture expanded, my experiences in Central and South America led me to regional writers: Mario Vargas Llosa, Luis Borges, and especially Gabriel García Márques. I had been to places like his fictional Macando and had begun to understand and appreciate the unique ethic that defined life in the heart of the region.

I began using a still camera in the late 70s to complement the films I had begun to make. In 1982 I contracted with a publisher in Mexico City to produce a film series about the origins of modern Mexico called Albores. It was a dream project that crashed the following year when the oil market, and the Mexican economy, tanked. But the Albores experience did generate lasting friendships, and it rekindled my affection for Mexico and the rest of Latin America. For the next three decades I returned again and again for work, for pleasure and just to be there. Always with a camera, always with my eye close to the ground to record the rhythms of life pulsating around me.

THE ANDES

In the 1970s you could hitchhike anywhere. And you could work most anywhere, too, if you weren't particular about the job. I spent a year hitching around Europe, working every so often to make the trip last longer. Before coming back to the U.S. I was staying in Eltham, a suburb of London, with a friend I'd traveled with in Scandinavia, and he was telling me about being on the road in Turkey and Afghanistan. What he described was an exotic world very different from the US, Canada and most of Europe. And I wanted to experience what he had; but instead of the Middle East I wanted to go to South America. I kept thinking about that day in the desert at El Sásabel, and especially about that village between the border and Altár. I imagined that the further south I went the more places like that I'd find.

I spent two years in graduate school in western Massachusetts before that trip would finally happen. I got fed up with academia about the same time my first wife got fed up with the drug rehab program she'd been working for. So we geared up, loaded up the Volkswagen bus and drove to California. We left the bus at her sister's house in San Bernardino and hitchhiked east. The night before crossing the US border we slept in sleeping bags on the twelfth green of a golf course in Nogáles, Arizona. I have a phobia about tarantulas and had a theory that they wouldn't venture from their holes on the fairways and creep onto the manicured turf of the greens. At least I hoped they wouldn't. The next day we crossed the border at Nogáles and took a train south to Mazatlán, on the coast of the Gulf of California.

We got off the train in Mazatlán at daybreak the next morning. The train station there sits on a rise so that looking out you can see the city and the waterfront stretching out before you. As we walked out of the station we saw the first of a long succession of sights that would be daily reminders that we had entered a different world. The cone of light that the street lamps cast beneath them were solid black with tens of thousands of two inch long cucarachas. From our vantage point at the station we could see a progression of lamps, cones of light and black, circular masses stretching all the way down to the water, almost two miles away.

We spent the next two months traveling south through Mexico and into Central America. The idea was to get to South America via Panama then travel down the spine of the Andes to Tierra del Fuego. We spent Thanksgiving at Lake Atitlán in the Guatamalan highlands, listening to nighttime firefights between Mayan rebels and government troops in the civil war that wasn't supposed to exist. By Christmas we'd gotten as far as Panama City and stalled. There was supposed to be a link on the Pan American Highway that went from the Panama Canal into Colombia but, like so many other things in that part of the world, there was the official story and then there was the reality on the ground. So we changed gears and tried to go to Cartagéna in Colombia via Colón, the Panamanian port on the Caribbean coast, but the trade winds were blowing the wrong way and boat traffic was minimal. In the end we flew to Quito two days before the New Year, severely depleting our available cash.

As soon as we got to Quito I began looking for the Southern Cross, a constellation that appears in the night sky south of the equator. I'd become fixated on seeing the Southern Cross as a pre-adolescent watching *Victory at Sea*, a World War II television series about the war in the South Pacific. A piece of music by Richard Rogers called *Beneath the Southern Cross* was always used by the film makers to accompany footage of ships under way, crashing through waves, steaming from one place to another. I imagined myself, moving through time and space to that music, seeing the Southern Cross coming up on the horizon. Quito is right on the Equator, not nearly far enough south, so I never saw it there. In fact I never saw it until several weeks later, riding down the coast of Peru on top of a truck loaded with bags of anchovy meal.

Ambato

From Quito we went south to Ambato, a mid-sized city in the central highlands of Ecuador. Every town and village in Latin America, no matter how small, has a zocalo at its center. The zocalos in the bigger towns were usually parks with some kind of bandbox in the center. In the small towns and villages they were sometimes no more than a patch of green with a few benches, or like the village below El Sásabel, just a well. The zocalo in Ambato was of the big town variety. There were walkways from every direction converging in the center at an elaborate bandbox with wrought iron railings. Around the bandbox there were several wrought iron benches.

We'd developed a routine by then whereby we'd come into a town, find a place to stay, then go out and sit in the zocalo to get the feel of the place and the people. We got to Ambato on New Year's Eve, and by the time we found a room and got out to the zocalo it was late in the afternoon. There are two seasons near the equator: dry and rainy. In Ambato it was the middle of the dry season, which meant sunny and hot during the day but, because of the altitude, colder at night. It had been in the low 80sF that day, but as we sat on a wrought iron bench near the bandbox it was cooling down fast.

When we first sat down there was nobody around us. But after about five minutes we began to draw a crowd. Just a couple people at first: A middle aged woman and a man about the same age with a shopping bag. Then a few more people of various ages joined them. They gathered in front of us about ten feet away, not in any way threatening, murmuring among themselves, and just politely observing us. When the crowd grew to about thirty people a guy in his early twenties worked his way up to the front and began speaking to me in halting English. I answered him in Spanish, though he seemed to enjoy his new status as spokesperson and continued asking questions in English. 'Where had we come from', 'why were we here', 'how did we get here' evolved to more personal questions and, after they found out we were Americans, a lot of questions about life in the US. The questions kept coming up through the crowd for maybe half an hour, after which people began to get bored and move away. In the end, we stayed in Ambato for several days with our interrogator and his friends, getting to know the countryside by day and hanging out with them by night.

I didn't have a camera during that year in the Andes, but I did when I came back to Ambato with a film crew almost twenty years later. By then the villages had become poorer and only women and old men were left to tend the crops that sustained the villages in the highlands. The able bodied young men had gone down to the lowlands to work on the plantations and in Guayaquíl, the teeming port city on the Pacific coast. They would do what migrants everywhere do: menial labor for not much money, which they would send most of back to their families in the mountains.

Besides the absence of the young and middle aged men in the villages another striking difference from twenty years earlier was that all the rivers in the mountains ran brown with silt. Quéchua speaking people in the Andes had been terrace farming largely by hand for more than a thousand years. But in the 1970s and 80s US-based aid programs that featured cheap financing, tractors and fertilizers had transformed agriculture from traditional farming practices to methods better suited for bottomlands rather than the steep, rocky terrain of the Andes. The result for people in the mountain villages was indebtedness, rampant erosion and deepening poverty. And most of the llamas were gone. When I'd been there twenty years earlier they were everywhere: in fields, on the streets, behind houses... everywhere. The signature animal of the Andes had largely disappeared.

The film crew of which I was a part was documenting agricultural conditions in the mountains. One of the objectives of the project was to encourage a return to traditional farming methods. We spent a morning filming villagers in Tungurahua Province working a patch of terraced farmland in the manner of their ancestors. Later that day we went higher into the mountains to another village so remote that even the footpaths ended above it. No one spoke Spanish up there, so one of the women from our first location came with us to translate. There were no men in that village the day we were there, and as we set up our equipment and sound-checked the spokesperson for the group I was acutely aware of the vast gulf between our crew and the women who were watching us. It was more than just culture and language. It was the thousands of years of births and deaths and famines and wars in that place high in the mountains that separated us from one another. Though I never took the still camera out that afternoon, the images of that place, especially the faces of the women, remain in my memory.

El Pishtaco

In Andes folklore a pishtaco is a blond, white man who creeps into villages at night and abducts, cuts the throats of and dismembers unsuspecting villagers. He then extracts the fat from the corpses and uses it to grease his machines. Spanish missionaries were suspected of being pishtacos who would kill people, boil down their fat, and use it to oil their church bells. The legend derives from the time of the conquistadores and suspicion of outsiders, especially Caucasians, persists to the present day. International assistance programs, like US Food for Peace, have been rejected by several communities on the altiplano near Lake Titicaca for fear that their real purpose was to fatten children and extract their fat.

I learned about pishtaco in Peru while hiking in the mountains near Ayacúcho, in the central highlands. I came up on a woman gathering firewood and loading it into her manta, an all-purpose cloak used to carry children, produce and everything else that needs to be transported. As I passed I greeted her in Spanish. As I did she looked up from what she was doing, stared right at me, and hissed. Then she picked up her manta, slung it onto her back and hurried away. Ayacúcho has a reputation for being hostile to outsiders. At that time it was still a sleepy provincial town, but later, in the 1980s, it was ground zero for El Sendero Luminoso (The Shining Path), a Maoist group that terrorized the central Peruvian highlands. At the height of its power the Sendero had extended its influence as far as the suburbs of Lima, but after the destruction of its leadership in the early 90s it devolved into drug trafficking. Its popularity among rural people in the central highlands derived in part from the same mistrust and fear of outsiders inherent in the pishtaco legend. And in the Quéchua and Aymara speaking areas of Ecuador, Peru and Bolivia that mistrust is very much alive.

The Train from Rio Bamba

In the 1970s in the Andes you could ride on top of the trains. You'd buy a third class ticket and you could either ride in an overfull compartment with people, produce and poultry or you could climb up onto the roof. The railroad people nailed 2x12 planks to the spine of the cars, so that's where you sat. At that time the trains were drawn by steam locomotives, the kind that belched clouds of smoke and cinders from the burning coal that fueled their power. When the train would come to a tunnel you had to do three things: take a deep breath, cover your nose and mouth with a bandana, and duck. The tunnel would fill with the noxious smoke from the engine and, if you were lucky, it would end before you had to breathe in again. If you were in one of the cars and the windows were open, which they often were, smoke would fill the car and not clear for several minutes after the train emerged from the tunnel.

We boarded the train to Guayaquíl in Rio Bamba, about 100 km south of Ambato. We bought third class tickets, but we rode inside to start because the train had to climb up to almost 15,000 feet to pass through the Andean mastiff before descending to the coast. As we climbed we passed through several villages and stopped in one before we came up to the pass. We were at about 11,000 feet and the weather had turned from cool and pleasant in Rio Bamba to gray and cold when we stopped. At that time the trains were rolling shopping malls, filled with people going down to the coast or to points in between, carrying with them whatever they had to sell. Every time the train would stop people from whatever town it was would board the train and commence doing business.

At every stop both sides of the train would be lined with makeshift tables and women selling hot food. Steaming bowls would be handed up to hands reaching out of the windows of the train and money would be handed down. Everyone seemed to know when the train was going to leave because they would conclude their business, the women from the tables would come on board to collect their bowls and the train would shortly thereafter be under way.

One day, on another train in Peru, I watched a woman across the aisle from me negotiate the price of her small goat with another woman who was standing next to the train below her window. I could only see the hat and eyes of the woman next to the train and hear them negotiating in Quéchua. As they arrived at a price acceptable to both of them the train lurched a little bit and began to move. As it did the woman across from me pulled a scale out from under her manta, weighed the goat so the woman outside could see the scale, and hoisted the goat out the window. The woman below took the goat and, running along side, handed up the money as the train began to pick up speed.

On all the trains in second and third class people would be moving through the cars selling things, playing flutes and guitars, and otherwise soliciting. Just before we got into the pass two middle-aged men came into our car. One of them had his eyes tightly shut and appeared to be blind. The other man was holding onto his arm and guiding him down the aisle that was cluttered with the belongings of people in the seats. When they got to about the middle of the car they stopped. The blind man took off his hat and handed it to his companion. Then he began to sing. He sang unaccompanied, so he kept the beat by pulling on his right earlobe in time with his voice. His songs were in Quéchua, so I didn't understand the lyrics. But they had the kind of power you can feel when you witness something beautiful that comes at you from a wholly unexpected place. When he finished singing his companion handed his hat to the person sitting nearest them. The hat went up and down the car for a few minutes, and then back with whatever cash it held. Then the companion emptied the hat, gave it back to the singer, took him by the arm and together they navigated their way to the next car.

El Náriz del Diablo (The Devil's Nose)

The Andes are steep. Along the coast of Peru, as the crow flies, they climb from the Pacific to over 20,000 feet in less than 100 km. In Ecuador they're further from the coast but just as steep. On the train route from Rio Bamba to Guayaquíl the railroad company that laid the track chose the shortest distance between two points, which meant going over a 30 km stretch called The Devil's Nose. The pitch along this stretch was too steep for the trains to go straight up or down, so when laying the track they installed a series of switchbacks to even out the grade. When the train would reach a particularly steep area the track would level out and come to a dead end. There would be a switch in the track along this level stretch, and when the last car on the train had passed over the switch the brakeman would radio the engineer who would then stop the train. The brakeman would throw the switch and the train would descend slowly in reverse down to the level below. It would proceed in this manner, backward and forward, until it had descended past the steep area. In the descent to Guayaquíl there were several of these switchback areas.

I sent descriptions of the switchbacks: how they were built and how they worked, back to my friend Ernie Berry who lived on Osprey Island in Raquette Lake, New York. Ernie was over seventy by then and had never been out of the United States. He was from South Paris, Maine and did seasonal work: the Adirondacks in the summer, Florida in the winter, his whole adult life. He was a confident, pragmatic man who I once helped move a six-room log cabin nearly a hundred feet up onto a point on the island where he lived. He had devised this complex array of house jacks, pulleys and blocks and tackles to do this, and could probably have done it by himself if I hadn't been there. His window to the world was National Geographic magazine, and he would talk about articles that interested him, which were usually about large construction projects somewhere in the world. I told Ernie before I left for Latin America that I would do two things: send him descriptions of things that I would see and, most specifically, go to the Panama Canal, see it in operation, and report back. I sent him several letters that year: about the Canal, crossing the Amazon in a dugout, the forty pound rainbow trout and foot and a half long frogs in Lake Titicaca, the switchbacks and other things I thought would interest him. And I told him about the Boca del Toro.

La Boca del Toro (Mouth of the Bull)

In the mountain towns in Peru nearly everyone chewed coca leaves or drank the máte made from coca leaves. A bag of leaves in the public markets the size of a basketball cost less than five US cents at that time and would come with a lump of lime paste that served as alkaline to extract the cocaine from the leaves. You would put some of the paste between your lower lip and your bottom teeth with your finger, then take a mouthful of leaves and chew. After a while you'd feel a tingling in your mouth and a real or imagined lift of your spirit. Quéchua people, particularly at higher altitudes, chew it as a hedge against hunger and fatigue.

The climate, terrain and soil in Leonócio Prado Province in the Huanúco District of Peru are perfect for growing coca plants. In the 1980s the region and its capital, Tingo Maria, would become synonymous with the cocaine trade that reached from the central Andes to the streets of major American cities. But in the 1970s Tingo was still a small, remote town halfway between Lima and the Amazon basin.

Heading north and east from Tingo the land falls away gradually at first, but beyond the town of Luyando the pitch gets steeper and the road more precarious. The Pacific side of the mountains in Peru is mostly desert, but on the Amazon side the vegetation gets denser and denser as you lose altitude and descend into the rainforest.

We came through Tingo Maria with the intention of going to Pucállpa, 250 km into the rainforest on the Ucayali River. The idea we had was to hitch a ride on a riverboat bound for Iquítos, the isolated jungle city downriver at the junction of the Ucayali and Amazon Rivers. We'd heard about the boats and traveling on the rivers back in Panama City from people who knew other people who had done it.

We boarded a full bus late in the day in Tingo with the expectation that we'd be in Pucállpa around midnight. What we didn't know at the time was that torrential rains had destroyed the stretch of road between Luyando and Aguaytía, the mid part of the trip down to Pucállpa.

We came to the first break in pitch darkness about 10 PM and the bus just stopped. The school bus type door opened and the driver and a few other people went out into the night. After a while I got up from my seat and followed them. Outside in the dark I followed the beam from a flashlight held by someone in a group that was gathered on the road about fifty feet ahead. As I approached the group I asked what was wrong. The answer came back, "no puede pasar", we couldn't pass. I asked why not and the answer was, "porque no hay carratera", because the road is gone. At that the guy with the flashlight took me by the arm and said, "cuidádo" while carefully walking me about fifteen feet ahead to where the road appeared to end. When we got to the jagged edge of the hardtop where the road had dropped away he shined his light down into nothing but darkness.

When we got back to the group I asked the driver whether we would go back to Tingo for the night. He said no, we would wait until morning when they would come and fix the road. I didn't see the point in arguing with him so I went back to the bus, climbed onto the roof and waited until dawn.

At first light I came down from the roof, walked to the edge of the abyss and looked down. The break in the road was about thirty feet wide. A rockslide had come down from the steep slope above and had taken a section of the road with it. About twenty feet below the edge of the break was a pile of rocks, roots and other jungle debris from the slide. It was clear to me that the bus wasn't going anywhere that day or any day soon thereafter.

Despite the interruption caused by the break we decided to go to Pucállpa anyway. We strapped on our packs and carefully climbed up well above the break, crossed over to beyond the rockslide and came back down onto the road. We thought we would find trucks somewhere nearby that were coming up from the lowlands and got blocked by a rockslide, too. When we did we could tell them the story of the road break and hitch a ride down to Pucállpa.

After an hour or so of walking and seeing no trucks we came to the second rockslide. This time debris was piled high directly on the road, making it impassable in either direction. We climbed up the slope as we had for the first break, crossed beyond the slide and came back down on the road. Again, no trucks.

We walked for several hours after that, crossing one rockslide after another, seeing almost no one other than an occasional straggler from the bus. We were by then several hundred feet above the Aguaytía River looking straight down a sixty-degree incline into raging floodwaters. A middle aged mestizo woman who we recognized from the bus walked with us for a time, before stopping at one of the few houses along that stretch of road. What I found remarkable about her, other than that she talked almost not at all, was that she was wearing flip-flops to navigate that rough terrain.

After a time the road began to descend and approach the banks of the river. That day we had learned from a local that the river flowed through a narrow pass with towering rock walls on both banks. There were two bridges that crossed the river, one before the pass to the opposite side from where we were and one that crossed back downriver from the pass. The locals called this stretch of river La Boca del Toro, the Mouth of the Bull.

We got to where the first bridge was supposed to be but found only ruined concrete stanchions and twisted steel rebar sticking up on both banks. From where we stood we could see down through the pass that the second bridge was gone, too. By then it was getting to be late in the day, so the prospect of walking back to where we had left the bus in the dark wasn't an option. And the idea of sleeping on the ground in that place made my tarantula phobia on the golf course pale by comparison. Then we saw our friend from the bus traversing the slope above us, walking in the direction of the pass.

She gestured to us to climb up to where she was then turned and kept walking. As we stepped into the brush beside the road and began the climb I thought about her flip-flops and wondered whether she had found better footwear when she stopped back at that house beside the road.

When we got up to where she had been standing there was a worn path heading in the direction she had gone. We followed the path for a short ways and saw that it disappeared into what looked like a cave entrance. Since the woman who had gestured to us was nowhere to be seen we assumed that she had followed the path into the mountain.

As we approached the mouth of what we thought was a cave we saw that it was instead the entrance to a tunnel. It was no more than eight or ten feet wide with a floor to ceiling clearance of maybe seven feet. It had clearly been built for foot traffic as a way through to the other side of the river gorge.

The floor was flooded with about six inches of water from all the recent rains, and as I reluctantly stepped into it I saw something moving above me. Hanging from the ceiling of the tunnel were what I perceived to be hundreds of very large bats. We could see a faint glimmer of light at the point where the tunnel turned to the right, which meant that it did go through to an actual exit. With no other real options open to us we bent down below the bats and silently stepped into the water in the tunnel.

Barely breathing, we passed through the tunnel, the whole time aware of the seething mass above us. The light grew stronger as we approached the end of the tunnel but, just as we were beginning to relax and breathe again, the exit came into full view. Less than a hundred feet beyond the exit was the mouth of another tunnel. This time we didn't hesitate but rather plunged straight ahead and through the second tunnel.

When we emerged from the second tunnel we could see the trucks that we had been hoping to see after each break in the road. They were lined up next to a series of shacks on a bank above the river that raged below them. As we approached a group of what I guessed were truck drivers I called out, "Is anybody going back to Pucállpa?" They just grinned and looked each other, then one guy said, "No we're all going to Lima." I told them about what we had just come through… the washed out bridges, the rockslides, the breaks… and said that the road wouldn't be passable for months. The guy that said they were all going to Lima took me aside and said, "Look, Pucállpa is hot, it's cooler up here. We have food, we have beer," and gesturing toward the shacks by the river, "we even have women up here. We're staying put."

Later we found two government agents who were on an inspection tour in a big open jeep that offered us a ride to Pucállpa. On the way down we stopped in the town of Aguaytía to distribute bags of US surplus rice to residents that lined up to receive it in ankle deep mud in the town zocalo. The river had only recently receded from the town and the expressions on the faces of the people as they took the rice were of both shock and gratitude.

When we left Aguaytía there was a large, live turtle on the floor of the jeep. One of the agents had bartered for it and said that he was taking it for his brother, who had a small pension in Pucállpa and would use it to make soup for the guests. He also said that, if we wanted, we could probably stay at the pension. We arrived at his brother's place well after dark. He offered us a room that was screened on three sides with geckos climbing on the screens. More than twenty-four hours after we'd left Tingo Maria we went to sleep in Pucállpa to the night sounds of the rain forest and the pungent smells of the Ucayali River.

The Twenty Sucre Note

As we descended through the switchbacks on the Náriz de Diablo the weather grew warmer, and by then we were riding on top of the train. Through the last of the switchbacks, while the train slowed to a crawl, we would walk along the spine of the cars, jumping from one car to the next. Forty years later that's hard to imagine, but the memory of it is palpable.

When we got down onto the coastal plain the weather turned hot and the landscape was wet from the previous day's rain. By now we were in Los Rios Province and had been stopping in different towns along the way, but never long enough in any of them for serious commerce to commence. But when we got to a town near the Caracól River the food tables were lined up along the tracks and people were milling around in anticipation.

When the train stopped the people waiting alongside the tracks came on board, passengers got off and the station area was transformed into a shopping plaza. From our perch atop the train we could watch everything unfolding below. After about fifteen minutes it became clear that we weren't going to move for a while. The initial flurry of activity below had begun to slow, and after another ten minutes or so the area around the train began to thin out. There were a couple of food tables below us but their owners were either on the train or otherwise absent from our view.

There was a small, open plaza in front of where our car had stopped. At the far side of the plaza, about a hundred feet from us, was a bar. At the entrance to the bar were swinging saloon doors, the kind you see in all the westerns: about a foot and a half of clearance from the ground and chest high on an average adult male at the top. When the plaza was all but deserted two guys came out of the bar and walked over to a spot just below us. They conferred for a few seconds then commenced to do something between them that we couldn't quite see. After a few minutes they emerged with what they had been preparing: a twenty-súcre note (about $5 US at the time) attached to what appeared to be a length of kite string.

They proceeded to place the note on the ground below us and then receded back in the direction of the bar, playing out the string as they went. When they reached the bar they went inside the saloon doors and waited, every so often peering over the top to see if someone had risen to the bait.

After a few more minutes a Quéchua woman with a small child in her manta walked by and stopped when she saw the twenty-súcre note. I could see the guys in the bar peering over the doors and watching her. As she bent down to pick up the note, the child riding up on her shoulders, they jerked the string and moved it just beyond her grasp. With only a slight hesitation she took a half step forward and bent down a second time to get the note. As she did they jerked the string again and moved it beyond her grasp. This time she caught on to the game. She stood up to look around and saw the two guys behind the door of the bar, who by now were laughing hysterically and yanking the bank note back to where they were. The woman commenced to yell at them in Quéchua and simultaneously follow after the retreating bank note. The note got there first and disappeared into the bar along with its owners. The woman who, with a child in the manta on her shoulders, went crashing through the swinging doors behind them following it.

The Coca Train

In the Andes trains were our preferred means of transportation when they went where we wanted to go. But in some of the more remote areas where they went you couldn't rely on the schedules. At the time there were two trains from Cusco to Machu Pícchu, the "Lost City of the Incas." There was the Quéchua train that stopped at every town along the Urubamba River all the way to Quillabamba in the lowlands, and one that went express only to Machu Pícchu and back. The Quillabamba train was pulled by a steam engine and consisted of mostly boxcars and a few old passenger cars. The express train was much newer, faster, air-conditioned and three times the price. It was for tourists to Machu Pícchu.

Machu Pícchu was only "lost" to the conquistadors because the Incas never revealed to them, or anyone else after that, where it was. The local Quéchua knew but kept the location to themselves until early in the twentieth century when a team of American historians started looking for Inca ruins along the Urubamba. The city was built in about 1450 as an estate for one of the last Inca emperors before the Spanish Conquest. It was abandoned a century later after the Conquest, possibly because its population was devastated by smallpox brought by the Spaniards.

As a general rule we avoided tourist areas, but we wanted to see Machu Pícchu. So we boarded the Quéchua train early one morning, along with high altitude farmers taking their products to the Quillabamba market and low altitude farmers who had sold out in Cusco and were going home. People around Cusco, at over 11,000 feet, grow temperate things like carrots and potatoes.

Quillabamba, at 3000 feet, is hot, wet and suitable for growing tropical fruits and vegetables. The markets compliment each other nicely, and the train is the conduit that facilitates the trade.

We got off the train next to the Urubamba directly below Machu Pícchu. The ruins are on a plateau 2000 feet above the river, so the only way to get there for the Inca was to climb straight up. There was a very curvy road to the top that was built in the 1920s and old beat up "cabs" that would take you up there for a price. The cabs had gotten there by train because there's no road next to the Urubamba, and the drivers charged whatever the market would bear, which was a lot. So we walked.

We found a well-traveled footpath in the jungle and followed it in our climb up to the ruins. Several hours later we emerged from the jungle. There was a small, newly built hotel near the ruins, which were in various stages of restoration. Nowadays it's reportedly the most visited tourist destination in South America, but back then it was still relatively primitive. There were few other people around while we were there, so we could wander silently around in the ruins and imagine life a half a millennium earlier before the Spaniards.

When we walked down from Machu Pícchu we boarded the Quéchua train down to Quillabamba, which at that time was the end of the line. And once we got there we couldn't get out. Every day for three days the guy in the shack that served as the rail depot would tell us there would be a train sometime that afternoon, and every day there wasn't. It was a hot, dusty town with no place to stay but one small hotel with rooms that had ceiling fans and armies of cucarachas that would scatter when you turned on the light. On the fourth day the railroad guy came out of his shack and pointed to some cars that were lined up on a sidetrack. He sold us third class tickets to Cusco and told us to go over and get into the last one in the row, which was an old cattle car. It was badly beat up with years worth of encrusted animal and vegetable matter on the floor and clinging to the walls. In one corner was a hole in the floor about the size of a toilet and, we guessed, for that purpose. We sat down on the ground outside the car with some other passengers, along with their chickens and goats for transport. About two hours later a train with about twenty cars switched onto our track and began backing up to connect to our string of cars.

After another hour the train finally began to move. There were no seats in the cattle car so we could either stand or sit on our packs. About ten kilometers out of Quillabamba we stopped, seemingly for no reason. Nobody ever closed the door to our car, so I could lean out and see what was going on outside and up ahead. There were several guys with machetes carrying bales of coca leaves out of the jungle and loading them into several of the cars ahead of ours. After a while the train began to move again, but only for another few kilometers before stopping again for another load of coca leaves. This went on all afternoon until just about dark. About then it began to rain.

The rain got heavier as we moved up the Urubamba Valley and conditions inside the cattle car began to deteriorate. About an hour after dark we pulled into the village of Santa Terésa and stopped. By then we'd gone about fifty kilometers in four hours. After a while the engineer passed the word that he was having mechanical difficulties and we'd be staying in Santa Terésa until another engine could come down from Cusco. Which meant we were there for the night.

Santa Terésa is a tiny town with three streets running parallel to the Urubamba. They step up on a steep grade until the top street is maybe a hundred feet above the river. Two or three cross streets ran right down to the water. The rail bed was uphill from the top street on a narrow plateau built by the railroad company. All the streets in the town were dirt and gravel and, since it had been raining heavily for most of the day there, were by now thick with mud. On the top street there was an informal restaurant set up in one of the houses facing downhill. The uphill side of the street was the desirable side to be on because you could step up out of the mud to get in the door. On the downhill side when you opened the door the mud came into the house. Other than the rail depot and the police station the restaurant was the only public place in town.

Stranded in Santa Terésa, we went looking for a place to get out of the rain. It was only about 8:00 but most of the houses in the town were already dark. On the top street the mud was ankle deep and the lights in the restaurant were the only ones still lit. There were a half dozen tables in the restaurant occupied by people from the train, and one by the local constable and his friend. The constable looked very official, sitting straight in his chair as he looked solemnly around the room. He nodded at us knowingly as we stepped inside and sat down at a table in the corner.

He let us settle in then walked over and asked if he could sit down. He was very young, maybe early twenties, had an open, friendly face and a deferential manner. He explained that there was no place to stay in Santa Terésa and asked us if we wanted to come back with him to the police station and sleep there.

It was still raining as we took the short walk along the top street from the restaurant to the police station. The station was at the end of the street and consisted of three rooms: an office with a wooden desk, a few chairs and a national flag mounted on the wall; and two smaller rooms that you entered from the office. The one room was the constable's sleeping quarters and the other one was the jail. We were sleeping in the jail.

It was a small room with a dirt floor, one tiny window and a heavy wooden door that could be bolted from the outside. The important thing was it was dry. After we rolled out our sleeping bags the constable came to the doorway and told us if we wanted to wash up to follow him into the office. As we did he walked past his desk to a side door that led outside. He turned to see if we were watching then flung open the door with a dramatic gesture. Outside, about fifteen feet away from the building was a cascading waterfall. He looked at us with a big smile on his face and said, "Pueden lavarse por aqui." You can wash up here.

When we came back inside he asked if either of us wanted to use the 'guest house'. By that he meant the bathroom. I said I did, thinking that there was an outhouse somewhere in back of the station. At that he walked over to his desk, took an enormous, old-fashioned key out of the middle drawer and indicated that I should follow him.

We walked through the mud down one of the cross streets that led to the river. When we reached the bottom we turned right and walked along the street closest to the water. On our left were a row of small buildings that cantilevered out over the now raging Urubamba. He walked over to the front of one of the buildings, took out the key he'd taken from his desk and opened one of the largest padlocks I'd ever seen. Then he stepped aside and gestured that I should go inside and do whatever it was I needed to do.

Inside it was a completely empty room about the size of a large kitchen. After my eyes adjusted to the light I looked around to see if there was something in the room that would require such a huge padlock. As my eyes adjusted further I noticed some light reflected off the river coming up through a hole in the floor in one corner of the room on the side that was hanging out over the river. It was a hole about the same size as the one in the corner of the cattle car, and for the same apparent purpose.

We'd met friendly policemen before in rural Peru. At the time the police were actively looking out for travelers like us and would try to help us out when they could. Thinking they could help travelers stranded on the destroyed road between Luyando and Aguaytía, I went to the police station in Pucallpa the day after we got there. I told the local captain the story of the rockslides, the gaps in the road and the washed out bridges. He listened politely and when I'd finished he smiled and said, "This is a poor country, people have to look out for themselves."

Tarjétas Santos (Holy Cards): Quito, Ecuador

This street vendor is selling holy cards, mostly to older women going in and out of the church behind him. He sets up in the morning before the early Masses and spreads out the cards. He told me no one ever steals the cards because "God would punish them and they know it."

Calle Espéjo: *the center of Ambato, Ecuador*

El Viéjo: *Tungurahua Province, Ecuador*

Las Campañeras: *Tungurahua Province, Ecuador*

Transportes: *Tungurahua Province, Ecuador*

People from the mountain villages take produce from the fields to markets in Ambato and Quito. They ride in the backs of camionetas (adapted pickups) and trucks with tarped-over beds to protect passengers and cargo from the weather.

El Pishtaco: *Tungurahua Province, Ecuador*

Las Yerbas (Herbs): Los Rios Province, Ecuador

Campesino*: Tungurahua Province, Ecuador*

Una Madre*: Los Rios Province, Ecuador*

Machu Pícchu: *Cusco Province, Peru*

The first photo taken of Machu Pícchu after the city was cleared of forest growth by the Hiram Bingham party in 1912.

El Abuelo*: Tungurahua Province, Ecuador*

Los Lustrabotas (Shoeshiners): *Quito, Ecuador*

In Latin America poor kids work on the streets. They sell gum, shine shoes, run errands and hustle the vendors in the markets. These lustrabotas are working the Sunday crowd in the zocalo in Quito, the capital of Ecuador.

GUAYAQUÍL

At that time there were a lot of people like us on the road: people with little money, knapsacks, and a willingness to travel close to the ground. The people like that we encountered in Latin America were mostly Europeans, Canadians, Australians and Mexicans. There were a few other Americans, too, and an occasional Asian. We would see the same people turn up at different junctures: hitchhiking, cruising the market in some town or on a train bound for the same place we were going. We would trade stories and information about places to stay and sometimes travel together for a while. We'd spent Christmas with some of the people we'd later see on the road at a sports complex outside Panama City that had been built for the Pan American games. We'd all been en-route to South America and had gotten stranded there for the holidays because of packed planes, boats that couldn't sail and a road that didn't exist. Sympathetic police in the city had opened the largely unused complex for travelers like us and put word out on the street that it was available. We spent Christmas Day swimming in the Olympic sized pool and feasting on the booty that we'd fanned out across the city to find the day before.

When we left the States part of the plan had been to go to the Galapagos Islands. The Galapagos are part of Ecuador but are about 1000 kilometers out into the Pacific from the mainland. The least expensive way to get there, we thought, would be to go to the port city of Guayaquíl and find a boat to go to the Islands. In Panama City two Norwegian guys who had been there confirmed that point of view. So when we got off the train in Guayaquil we went to the zocalo to find someone who knew about the boats.

Guayaquíl is a hot, crowded, dusty city. The zocalo is pungent with tropical odors that permeate everything and populated by dozens of large iguanas in the trees, some of them more that two feet long. Old men play chess and checkers on the concrete boards set up around the center. We found that the preteen lustrabotas (shoeshiners) that cruise the zocalo in Latin cities were generally a good place to start looking for information. So we sat on a bench under a large shade tree and waited for them to find us. Two large iguanas lay motionless on a branch above us.

When we asked for information from kids on the street we'd learned that what we got might or might not be accurate, but it would always be entertaining. The lustrabota that pointlessly worked on my scuffed up work boots did not disappoint. He told us to go see his uncle in the market and that he could connect us with a boat to the Galapagos.

The public market isn't far from the zocalo. When I returned to Guayaquil with the film crew it was much as I had left it twenty years earlier. It was still a vast, sprawling thing where you could find virtually anything you can imagine. Centered in a designated area, it spills out into the streets with smells that are a composite of hanging raw meat, burning charcoal, over-ripe fruit and the remains of past markets that have been ground into the street. People are everywhere: working, talking, looking, telling stories and negotiating prices.

We found the lustrabota uncle standing next to a table piled high with cheap children's toys. Yes, he could connect us with a supply boat going to the Galapagos, but it wouldn't be leaving for two weeks. Did he know of any other boats that were going sooner? Yes, he said, "pero cuesta mucho", but they were expensive; too expensive for us, as we found out after checking with a travel office near the market. So we did what we often did when presented with an unworkable plan: we made a new plan. Instead of waiting two weeks for a cheap way to the Galapagos we boarded a night barge to Peru.

The barge was very cheap and very slow. By water it was only about 100 miles from the port of Guayaquíl to Tumbes, the entry point in Peru, but it took until sunrise the next day to get there. The barge was hauling cocoa and rice from the plantations north of Guayaquil, and took on a handful of passengers to fatten the bottom line. We slept in hammocks rigged up on the deck, and pulled our packs into the hammocks for extra security.

We found a ride from the barge to a tiny village about 100 km south of Tumbes called La Cruz. In La Cruz we ate fresh caught fish by gaslight on the back porch of a small restaurant overlooking the Pacific. That night we walked a couple hundred meters down the beach and rolled out our sleeping bags above the high tide line. Around first daylight I heard voices coming from the direction of the ocean. The water was calm and the small, breaking waves did little to mute them.

After a while, coming through the mist toward the beach, a wooden raft with people on board began to take shape.

There were three boys on the raft, two of them about twelve and the third a little older, and they'd been fishing. They pulled the raft through the surf and up onto the beach. There were a few fish on the raft and I asked what they were going to do with them. "We'll sell them to Doña Francesca at the restaurant", the oldest one said, "we do it every day the sea is calm enough for us to go out." With that they took the fish from the raft and walked off down the beach toward the restaurant.

It was a short walk from the beach back to the road south. That day we were in luck; we managed to hitch a ride in the open bed of an anchovy truck that would take us all the way to Lima. Two or three nights later, somewhere between Chimbóte and Lima, lying between thirty kilo bags of dried anchovies, I finally got to see the Southern Cross, rising off the horizon to the south and west, out over the Pacific. At night, when the driver got tired of driving, he would pull over somewhere near the ocean. We had hollowed out a nest for ourselves on top of the truck by piling some anchovy bags on top of each other. Those nights on the truck we went to sleep hearing the rhythm of the waves and woke up to the sound of pelicans feeding in the surf.

From Lima we took the train up to Huancayo, and from there south through Ayacúcho and Abancay, all the way to Cusco. From the window of a bus traveling on a windy mountain road above Abancay, I remember seeing a tarantula in the road that was so big that I could make out all of its features while going by at 40 miles per hour. Or maybe it was my phobia that remembers it that way.

From Cusco and the Coca Train we went south again, to the Altiplano, Lake Titicaca and into Bolivia. I wrote Ernie letter after letter: about the witches market and the bullet holes in the walls of city hall in La Paz, about eating llama meat at two AM outside the market in Puno and about walking up hills and trying to breathe at the same time at 13,000 feet. To be sure they'd get there I would save the letters and mail them at the Canadian Consulate whenever we were in a town big enough to have one.

When we got back to the States one of the first things I did was call Osprey Island. I imagined going up there and sitting by the stove with Ernie and sharing my adventures with him. His wife Alice answered the phone. I asked if Ernie had gotten my letters and was he around and could I talk with him. There was a pause at the other end, and then, in her down east accent, Alice said, "Ernest died last wintah." I never went back to the Island.

El Zocalo: *Guayaquíl, Ecuador*

Juego de Damas (Checkers): *Guayaquíl, Ecuador*

These men were passing the time in the public market playing checkers. The man on the left was the champion. The one on the right is the challenger.

Boletos de Loteria (Lottery Tickets): *Guayaquíl, Ecuador*

The man in the foreground is selling sandals and lottery tickets. As the shot was being set up for him the other vendors in the vicinity took notice and posed as a group.

Se Vende Pollos: *Guayaquíl, Ecuador*

La Familia Maldonado

The Maldonado family has maintained a presence in the pubic market in Guayaquil for three generations.

MEXICO CITY

When I was growing up in the northeastern U.S. my only exposure to Mexico came from watching The Cisco Kid on TV. The Kid was a goodhearted outlaw played by an Hispanic actor named Duncan Renaldo. Cisco spoke okay English, albeit with an accent, but his partner, another Hispanic actor named Leo Carrillo, would say things in pidgin English like "come on Ceesco, let's went", that were meant by the Anglo scriptwriters to be funny. We were far from the borderlands of the southwest, so before Sásabe and the Sonoran desert portalled me into the actual place, my references to Mexico and Mexicans were Paramount backlots and the Kid. Two months on the ground, traveling from one end of the country to the other, going to and coming from Central and South America completely changed all that. Among other things I learned that Anglo and Latino views of the world are very different.

For instance, in the early 1980s the Argentine junta invaded the Falkland Islands. The Falklands are a couple hundred miles off the Argentine coast and have been claimed by Argentina ever since the British colonized them in the mid-nineteenth century. Indignation was running high in the non-Latin world at the effrontery of the Argentinians to dare challenge the British in such a blatant, hostile manner. The Argentine government characterised its military action as the reclamation of its own territory; the Brits considered it an act of war. In the U.S., TV news and newspapers expressed outrage and were sympathetic to the British. Public opinion polls reflected the media, showing over 90% of U.S. citizens siding with the Brits.

In Mexico it was exactly the opposite. In the middle of the ten week war I happened to be in Mexico City for the Albores project and was staying with a Mexican family. Mexican media and 95% of the Mexican public favored the Argentinian position while my hosts and all of their friends were revelling in what the Argentinians had done. In their view, by invading Las Malvínas (the Spanish name for the Falklands), the Argentinians had poked a finger in the imperialist eye and were sending a not subtle message north that, after a hundred and fifty years of being humiliated by the Monroe Doctrine, the days of acquiescence to Yankee control were over. Despite the fact that the Brits were eventually able to send the invaders back to the mainland, a message had been sent.

From the village of San Miguel Xicalco on its southwestern edge, you can see the whole south end of Mexico City. The village is located on a ridge a kilometer above the valley floor, which is already at 2140m (7000 ft). And you look directly across the Valley of Mexico at the towering twin volcanoes: Popocatepetl and Ixtaccihuatl, both nearly 18,000 above sea level.

The Mixtecs were the first people to settle the city in about 1325. They called it Tenochitlán. The original site was on an island in Lake Texcoco, which at that time comprised the entire Valley of Mexico. The Spaniards laid siege to and destroyed the city in 1521, minimized Lake Texcoco, and rebuilt it in accordance with Spanish colonial design. On its way to becoming one of the world's largest cities, La Ciudad de Mexico has absorbed village after village, reducing once-remote towns like San Miguel Xicalco to suburbs.

Caras (faces)

shot in a public market in the San Angel district of Mexico City. It displays the diversity of ethnicity and the dynamism inherent in the city's 30,000,000 inhabitants.

La Piñata

This girl is running through the frame in San Miguel Xicalco while her mother in the background tries to locate and hit the piñata strung on a wire above them. Not in the frame is a very large dog named Galeano that stole some of the candies as they fell to the ground when the piñata was shattered.

Recuerdo de tu Familia

In Mexico people believe that your ancestors are always with you. Cemeteries are gathering places for families bringing picnics and gifts for the departed, especially on El Dia de los Muertos (Day of the Dead) on October 31. This cemetery near San Miguel Xicalco is a recuerdo (remembrance) of Teodora Gomez de Alvaya.

Viva la Virgen

Small street level chapels are common in Mexico City and open to anyone that wants to walk in. In this chapel in the San Angel district of Mexico City the women were praying to Our Lady of Guadalupe.

Avenida 16 de Septiembre

When I first looked up at the sign in the background the little girl in the center was peeking over the wall and looking at me. While I set up the camera the other two older girls climbed up and sat on the wall, clearly wanting to be seen.

El P.R.I.

The Partido Revolutionario Institutional dominated Mexican politics for three quarters of a century through patronage, corruption and rigged elections. Party operatives plastered every available surface with posters and hand-scrawled inscriptions like the ones on the wall beside these two schoolgirls. The Party's reign ended in 2000 but it's presently making a comeback.

Globos (balloons)

Shot in Chapultepec Park. The Park is centered on the hill where Chapultepec Castle stood and is the largest municipal park in the western hemisphere. The Castle protected Mexico City from the west during the Mexican- American War. In September 1847 U.S. Marines stormed the castle and paved the way for the fall of the city.

Chucherías (trinkets)

OUTSIDE THE CAPITOL

Mexico is the 13th largest independent nation in the world. Comprised of thirty-one states and the Federal District, it stretches over two thousand miles from Tijuana to the Guatemalan border. It's 120,000,000 inhabitants speak some sixty-eight languages, most of them pre-Columbian, that endure in indigenous communities all over the country. The landscape varies from the hot, flat jungles of the Yucatan to the temperate, mountainous central part of the country, to the deserts of the north that border the United States.

The road south from Acapulco on the Pacific coast passes through a particularly remote part of the country. About 150 km south of Acapulco is the small town of Marquelia. On Sundays the main road through town is blocked by a sprawling market. People crowd up the area, buying and selling everything that's possible in that part of the world. Alongside the road there is a small sign mounted on a pole, Kodak yellow with red lettering that reads "Photo Marquelia". Passing through Marquelia one Sunday we became curious about the sign and followed a pot-holed street back through the village until we came to a thatched-roof palapa with the same red and yellow sign over the doorway. A guy dozing at a table inside awoke, looked up and saw two gringos staring at him. I asked if he was the photographer and he said, "No, the photographer is my brother." I said to tell his brother that I was an American photographer and wanted to meet him.

A few minutes later the photographer and his very pregnant wife came into the studio from a courtyard that connected it with their house. He had an incredulous look on his face as though he didn't quite believe that a foreign photographer could find him, tucked away as he was in a remote Mexican town.

He turned out to be the town chronicler. Weddings, funerals, special events; anything that merited a visual record, he was the guy that recorded it (this was way before I-phones). He had an inexpensive 35mm camera with one lens and a 4x5 studio camera that he used for document photos and portraits. He didn't have a darkroom (there was no potable water in Marquelia), so after a shoot he would take the bus to Acapulco to a lab there to develop his film and make his prints.

He admired the contents of my camera bag, mounting each lens and peering through the viewfinders of my Nikons. As I watched him I was acutely aware of how much we Americans take for granted. When we'd finished comparing notes about what we did and how we did it we spent the rest of the afternoon taking pictures, mostly of each other.

Caballero

Shot west of Mexico City in Mexico state, at a Sunday rodeo outside a small town. There were the usual rodeo events being held in a makeshift arena set up with several rows of bleachers around it. Inside and outside the arena people from around the area were dressed in formal hacienda attire. This guy's hat, monogrammed holster, chaps and carefully coiled lariat caught my eye.

Vaquéros (Cowboys)

The celebrated American 'cowboy' tradition was originally brought to North America from the Iberian Peninsula. It proliferated in the 17th and 18th centuries in Mexico and California when the latter was still part of Mexico. These vaquéros are celebrating that tradition at a Sunday rodeo near Valle de Bravo in Mexico state.

Rodeo

Formally dressed for the photo, this boy changed into dungarees and competed in the calf-roping event in the Sunday rodeo outside the village of Valle de Bravo in Mexico state.

La Centinela (the sentinal)

The woman in the alcove is the caretaker of this church in a village near Morelia in Michoacán.

La Madonna del Abarrote (Madonna of the Grocery Store)

Shot near San Cristóbel de Las Casas in Chiápas, in the south of Mexico bordering on Guatemala. There were several small children, two of them hers, running around the store during the shot. The camera was set on a counter that ran perpendicular to the one she's leaning on to steady it.

Zapateria (shoe store)

Shot from the roof of a pension looking out at the colonial silver mining city of Taxco in Guerrero state. This juvenile drama unfolding in the street outside the shoe store resolved with the dog getting the treat and the boys losing interest and walking away together.

Photo Marquelia

Niñitas (little girls)

Small cities and towns in Mexico are designed for walking. Commercial districts surround a zocalo or central park in the center of which, in the bigger towns, is a kind of bandbox. On Sundays families dress up and come to the zocalo to socialize. This shot is from one entrance to the zocalo in Cuernavaca. As luck would have it two little girls in white dresses chased each other through the frame.

Hombre de Depósitos (Deposits Man)

Mexicans consume an enormous quantity of bottled beverages. In Tehuacan, a small city in Puebla state, there is a building with a mountain of empty soda/water bottles in front. Most of the soda pop and bottled water consumed in the country at that time came in re-usable bottles that carried a bounty of a few centavos each. The proud owner of the business stood proprietarily by the front door. In Tehuacan, he was the "deposits man."

Palétas (Popsicles)

This was shot early on a Sunday morning when the streets of the old silver mining town of Taxco were still empty, except for this one vendor headed for the zocalo. Much of Mexico is hot and dry, so in the cities vendors fill the streets selling refrescos (soft drinks), aguas (fruit drinks made with water) and palétas.

Monastério San Gabriél

Cholúla is between Mexico City and Puebla and is known as "the city of churches". Families from both Spanish colonial cities built elaborate "chapels" there. This is the Franciscan Monastery of San Gabriél, built by monks in the 1540s over top of a destroyed temple to the Aztec God Quetzalcoatl. The missionaries originally tried to supplant indigenous beliefs with Spanish Catholicism, but over time the local religion evolved into a hybrid that borrowed the traditions of both the Aztecs and the Spaniards. The white pennants streaming from the belfry are typical adornments on churches in Mexico.

Dos Niños

In Mexico everyone drinks bottled water because you can't drink from the tap. When this was shot most of the bottled water in the country came from Tehuacán and Peñafiel, the springs that flow underground from Pico de Orizaba, the highest mountain in Mexico. Before colonial times Moctezuma had the waters of Peñafiel hauled to Tenochítlan for their special qualities. These two kids were playing futbol (soccer) in the street, not far from the entrance to Peñafiel.

La Catedrál de San Juan Compostéla

La Madonna del Mercádo (Madonna of the Market)

This young girl in the public market in Oaxaca was helping her mother sell fruits and vegetables that were spread out on blankets and stacked in piles. Her juxtaposition with the uniformed schoolgirl behind her is emblematic of Central and South America: the tension between the insular, traditional world of the pre-Spanish native people (indígenas) and modernity.

THE YUCATAN

Geographically, most of Mexico is mountains and deserts. The Yucatan peninsula is neither. It is mostly flat, lush and, in the northern part, dotted with deep ponds the native Mayans call cenótes. Mayan cities in the Yucatan were built near the cenótes because they were a source of fresh water. They were also used as sacrificial cites. The Mayans believed that they were gateways to the afterlife and would throw family valuables in them, hoping to reconnect with their ancestors after death.

During the mating season, the mangrove swamps on the northern coast are thick with American flamingos. Travelers come to the area to watch flocks of the odd pink birds wading in the swamps. The region is very poor and there are few window screens to keep out the swarms of mosquitoes that infest the area. Near Tizimín, from the protection of a car in which I was seeking refuge from a particularly aggressive swarm, I watched an old Mayan woman walk slowly and deliberately by me, through the mosquitoes, carrying a mattress on her back. I recall marveling about the toughness and resilience of the people there, and the Mayans in particular.

In 1847, after nearly three centuries of peonage, the Mayans rebelled against their Spanish overlords in what came to be known as the Caste War of the Yucatan. The capital of the rebellion was Chan Santa Cruz, now Felipe Caríllo Puerto, situated in the modern state of Quintana Roo, near Chetumál, close by the border with Belize. They outnumbered the non-Mayans by five to one in the region and formed a formidable force. By the 1850s they controlled most of the Yucatan, all the way from the Belizian border westward to the gates of Mérida and Campéche. The war officially ended in 1901, but resistance continued in Mayan villages until 1933.

Late one afternoon, heading west out of Felipe Caríllo Puerto in an old Volkswagen bug, a friend and I turned off the main road onto a dirt track in the direction of Dzula, the last Mayan village to resist the Mexican army in 1933. The smell of wood smoke hung in the air as we passed milpas (slash and burn agricultural fields farmed by the Mayans for centuries) still smoldering from fires lit by local farmers to prepare for the next year's crops.

Like most Mayan villages in the Yucatan, Dzula is poor. Unpaved streets lead to what serves as a zocalo at the center, comprised of some open space on which there was a wooden bench. Across from the open space there was a large cinder block building with an electric line that came in from the main road. We stopped in front of it, got out of the car, and waited. After a few minutes people began to gather.

Everyone in Dzuba spoke Mayan; less than half spoke Spanish. As a small crowd gathered around the car, a young man came to the front of it and asked in Spanish why had we come to the village. I said that we were curious about life in the small Mayan towns in the jungle and wanted to see for ourselves. He welcomed us to Dzuba and invited us to come into the nearby block building, explaining that the town used it as a meeting place. Inside we found ourselves standing among what seemed to be much of the village.

They sat us down on a wooden bench that was situated on a raised platform facing the crowd. The man who had invited us in served as the spokesperson, relaying questions up to us from the crowd. After a time a man came into the back of the room carrying a large crate. People cleared a path for him as he made his way up to where we were sitting. He set the crate down on the platform, stepped back, and looked at us, smiling expectantly. The spokesperson said in Spanish, "queremos mostrar algo a ustedes" (we want to show you something). With that he opened the crate and carefully picked up its content, a brown brocket deer, brought it over to us and placed it in my friend's lap. Brown brockets are small deer (20- 30 pounds) native to the jungles of the Yucatan. The one in my friend's lap was quivering but compliant. She raised her head as my friend stroked her ears, as he might have done to a puppy.

After a few minutes it was my turn to hold the deer. The whole time there was subdued chatter in the room in Mayan. Glances in our direction suggested they were talking about us. The man who brought the brocket deer in eventually took her from me, put her back in the crate and took her from the room. We answered more questions that came up from the crowd until, as it began to get dark, we stood up to leave. As we did a woman stepped in front of me and handed me a painting. It showed a Mayan warrior with his foot firmly implanted on the neck of a Spanish soldier. Above the warrior flew a large quetzal bird, another native of the Yucatan. The Mayans were still rebelling. We had spent the afternoon with the descendants of a people who, a hundred years before, had nearly pushed their colonial oppressors into the sea.

Restaurante La Villa: *Valladolid, Q.R.*

The boy in the center was cleaning up one morning while his two pals kept him company. At my request they climbed onto the chairs to stand in front of the "Superior" mirror.

Barco de Pescadór (Fishing Boat)

Moored in the surf in the Caribbean in Quintana Roo, off the west coast of the Yucatan Peninsula.

Adelbérto Pac, Descendant of Mayan Rebels

Mr. Pac was born in the town of Felipe Caríllo Puerto, the last stronghold of the Mayan insurgency against the Spaniards. He was working in a small hotel on the Mexican border with Belize when I met and befriended him. He told stories of his family's part in the rebellion with great pride. He stood for this photograph as a personal favor.

67

La Abuela: *A grandmother points out a large fish for her grandson and his friend. Shot at Lake Bacalar, north of Chetumál.*

Los Portáles (Doorways)

The courtyard of a colonial era pension in the city of Valladolíd. During the Caste War Valladolíd was occupied and sacked by Mayan rebels and all non-Mayans who did not manage to escape were killed. Later in the war, the city was retaken by Mexican government forces. In modern times the town is mostly a way station between Cancun and Merida.

Pension Rámos

BELIZE

When I entered Belize for the first time I had to give up my copy of that month's American Photographer magazine at the border. It had a photograph on the cover of Natasha Kinski, naked with a python wrapped around her, that got the attention of the customs officials. I was carrying a rucksack, which they opened and began removing my belongings… until they got to the magazine. There was a pause in their dialogue with me while they made comments to each other about the photograph. When I offered them the magazine as a gift they put my belongings back in the rucksack, closed it, stamped my passport and waved me through.

In the 1980s Belize was still mostly a tropical frontier. Contemporary eco-tourism was virtually unknown, and the main road from Corozál, the third largest town in the country, to Belize City was still dirt. Formerly British Honduras, it was a slave colony based primarily on sugar production until the British outlawed slavery in 1833. And it didn't become an independent country until 1981. After Hurricane Hattie leveled seventy-five percent of Belize City in 1961, a new city was built to house the capital at Belmopan, fifty miles to the east and off the coast. The Guatemalans consider Belize to be part of their country, so, after granting independence in 1981, the British maintained a military garrison to insure against Guatemalan incursion until 1994.

Belize City is poor and, as a legacy of being an old British slave colony, English-speaking and disproportionably black. As I was walking up to the road north to Orange Walk and Corozál I passed by a group of five or six black guys standing around and smoking in front of a house. As I passed one of them called out behind me, "White man." His tone was not friendly or unfriendly, just prolonged with the accent on "man", like "white maaaan…" I said back, in the same tone and cadence, "black maaaan…" and kept walking until I reached a place up the road that seemed like a good place to begin hitchhiking. I set my rucksack down and looked back at the group in front of the house. They had apparently lost interest in me and had moved on to another subject.

The man in a pickup who stopped for me said I was foolish to be doing what I was doing, especially at night (it was getting dark) and especially there. We talked a lot during the long, dusty trip to Corozál and we became friends. In fact he invited me to come to his house to meet his family. During the three days I spent with them they celebrated their son's fifth birthday. My present was a family portrait. Later, when I got back to my darkroom, I sent them some prints.

Machítos (Little Machos)

Kids run the streets of Belize City in packs like this one, sometimes on the hustle but mostly just being young. Most of what you see in this shot is kids having fun. But the one in front, despite his size, is very much into being a gangster.

La Familia Suárez

Un Gordo y Dos Flacos (A Fat Guy and Two Skinny Guys)

These men were standing around outside the house of the man on the left, near Corozál. The one on the right introduced him as El Gordo, (fat guy) though he didn't seem to appreciate it. They invited me in and we went behind the house into a shady grotto with geckos running along the walls and a large iguana in a tamarindo tree.

Barcos Pescadóres

Fishing boats moored on Ambergris Cay, Belize

EPILOGUE

After nearly a year in Mexico, Central and South America, we came up through Chihuahua and crossed back into the United States at El Paso, Texas. I had traveled all that time without a camera, the idea being that a camera was intrusive and when I took one out I would not be able to really connect with people. Many of the stories in "Corazón" are from that period. There are many other stories that I remember but do not have a visual record for: eighteen inch frogs on the shores of Lake Titicaca, so big that they would make a distinctive, 'splatting' sound as they fell from one rock to another in the dark; women chewing coca leaves in villages twelve thousand feet above sea level; dried llama fetuses in a witch's market in Bolivia; Quéchua speaking men with short, thick ropes that they used to lash crates of fruits and vegetables on their backs in the markets; landing in a sea plane on the Ucayali River in Peru and taxiing to a village by passing a dugout canoe with four tribal men, ceremonially painted, coming from the opposite direction. All in memory, none of it on film.

By the time I went to Mexico for the Albores project (see Introduction) I had been shooting professionally for five years, so I was comfortable with a camera in my hands. I took it to villages, markets, private homes; anywhere I happened to go. I also spoke enough Spanish to put people at ease when I took out the camera. The photographers I have always admired most are the ones able to capture images of unremarkable persons and events in remarkable ways.

We traveled in the style of Jack Kerouac's 'dharma bums'. We went to places just to see what was there. We had very little money. We hung small cloth bags with leather strings around our necks to hold our passports and whatever cash we had; to protect us from pickpockets. We stood in the rain for hours, waiting for rides. We got stranded for days at a time in places we'd never heard of before. We bought bags of coca leaves in the markets for a penny and chewed mouthfuls with lime paste like the Quéchua-speaking people around us. We slept in brothels, cheap pensions, police stations and on the backs of trucks.

There were a few Americans traveling as we did at that time, but most of the people we encountered were from other parts of the world. Many of them had been born during or just after the Second World War and had been profoundly affected by it, particularly the Europeans. I once expressed a fondness for a town in Germany to an Englishman. He looked at me oddly and then proceeded to tell me that he still hated Germans because of the war. "You're an American", he said, "your cities were never bombed."

People on the road were young, mostly in their twenties. I once met a man in his late fifties carrying a knapsack and wearing a red bandana tied around his head. He was staying in a cheap pension in Belize City at a time when the city was a dangerous place and few people went out after nightfall. But it turned out his son was working in the interior and was coming the next morning to pick him up.

There were a lot of wanderers, like the Coke Man. We called him that because he wanted to go somewhere where the CocaCola man had never been. At that time Coke, not fast food, was the symbol of the American cultural invasion. He wanted to avoid everything American. He was from Brooklyn and had been a Navy pilot, flying off carriers to bomb North Vietnam. The war had shaped his view of the world in a way that made him never want to go home again. He wore a long black coat in which he carried everything he owned. He had sewn extra pockets on the inside of the coat to hold his poncho, clothes and food he bought in the markets. He'd been traveling for five years by the time I met him and he was headed into the Amazon basin. He hoped the coke man hadn't been there yet.

Sásabe is very different now, on both sides of the US-Mexican border. People are less relaxed and more wary. That tiny village in the desert between Sásabe and Altár is probably different, too. Or maybe it only ever existed in my imagination. The vagaries of politics and economics have changed much in the region over time, but not the cultural essence. For me, that day in the desert, real or imagined, began an affair that continues unabated.

Self-Portrait: Belize City 1983

Printed in the United States
By Bookmasters